How to write what you want to say ... in business

a guide for those who know
what they want to say
but can't find the words

Lyn Carter and Patricia Hipwell

First published 2016

National Library of Australia Cataloguing-in-Publication entry

Creator:	Carter, Lyn, author.
Title:	How to write what you want to say ... in business : a guide for those who know what they want to say but can't find the words /Patricia Hipwell and Lyn Carter.
ISBN:	9781925236910 (paperback), 9781925522099 (ebook)
Subjects:	Business writing. Business presentations. Business communication.
Other Creators/Contributors:	Hipwell, Patricia, author. Cottier, Charlotte.
Dewey Number:	808.06665

Typeset in Delicious 10 pt.

Text and cover design: **Boolarong Press**

Image of *Pencil-pusher* by Zsuzsanna Kilian

Note: Text examples of the writing skill in business have been created to demonstrate that skill. Possible inaccuracies and out-of-date information in these texts are acknowledged by the authors and do not detract from the validity of their inclusion.

Published by Boolarong Press, Salisbury, Brisbane, Australia.

Printed and bound by Watson Ferguson & Company, Salisbury, Brisbane, Australia.

contents

dedication ... iv
introduction ... v
the nature of business writing ... vi
key terms and ideas defined ... 1

forms of business writing

- briefing note/paper ... 2
- business plan ... 4
- email ... 6
- envelope ... 8
- file note ... 10
- letter ... 12
- media release ... 14
- meeting notice (agenda) ... 16
- meeting record (minutes) ... 18
- memorandum (memo) ... 20
- newsletter ... 22
- proposal/submission ... 24
- report ... 26
- speech/presentation ... 28

employment

- employment (job) application ... 30
- job advertisement ... 32
- reference ... 34
- responding to selection criteria ... 36
- resume/curriculum vitae (cv) ... 38
- selection criteria ... 40

general principles of business writing ... 42
presentation – formats, styles and page layouts ... 44
style manuals and standard templates ... 46
modality ... 47
alternative action verbs ... 48
alternatives to 'said' ... 49
gender-neutral language ... 50
glossary ... 51
my notes ... 54
about the authors ... 58

dedication

To our mothers, Jean and Phyllis, our first literacy teachers.

introduction

This guide, written by Lyn Carter of Count on Numeracy and Patricia Hipwell of logonliteracy, provides the language needed to write for a variety of purposes:

- business and government communications, and
- employment decisions, including applicants, referees and selection panels

It aims to provide those with limited experience in these forms of writing with a starting point to say what they want to say using language that mature writers use.

The book is set out in a double-page format:

- The first page defines the purpose, audience, and things to know about the form of writing, and provides some useful vocabulary.
- The second page provides relevant sentence starters and an example of the skill in a short piece of writing (with the sentence starters shown in italics).

How to write what you want to say ... in business is a guide for those who know what they want to say but can't find the words. It provides a unique tool for improving writing. It seeks to assist inexperienced writers of business and government communications and also students of business and legal courses from the middle years of schooling to the tertiary level and beyond.

This book is the fifth in a series and takes a similar approach to:

How to write what you want to say by Patricia Hipwell

How to write what you want to say ... in mathematics by Lyn Carter and Patricia Hipwell

How to write what you want to say ... in the primary years by Catherine Black and Patricia Hipwell

How to write what you want to say ... at university by Patricia Hipwell and Lyn Carter

Another book is soon to be released:

How to write what you want to say ... in science by Malcolm Carter, Lyn Carter and Patricia Hipwell

the nature of business writing

'The wisest use of time is to think about what it is you want to say. Consequently, a systematic approach to writing demands that thinking about the topic should precede any attempt to get things on paper ... or on the screen.'

A government agency's advice to its employees on effective writing

The aim of this book is to assist that process of 'getting things in paper or on the screen'. It explains how to write in the styles used by most business, government and other organisations.

In many cases, the first contact an organisation has with its clients, customers, and prospective employees is in written form, for example through a website, advertisement, letters, reports, and brochures. Similarly, the first contact that most job applicants have with a future employer is in writing. People make judgements about an organisation or a job applicant based on the quality of their written communications. In some cases, documents produced by an organisation may be used as evidence in court. This means that appropriate and correct written business communications are vital.

The key features of business writing are that it

- conveys factual information, including evidence, where possible
- expresses ideas positively rather than negatively
- is structured, often using section headings
- has a formal or semi-formal tone
- is a precise and concise form of communication
- prefers active to passive voice
- uses everyday words that are familiar to the intended reader
- uses inclusive, non-discriminatory language
- avoids contractions and clichés
- may include illustrations and tables.

Although this book is about writing, the principles of effective business writing also apply to effective communication through speaking. In business, much of what we say is often written first, as a script or speaking notes for a speech. So, this book will also assist with spoken communication.

These ideas, and others, are developed throughout the book.

key terms and ideas defined

form of writing	the type or style of the text to be produced, for example, business letter, employment application or newsletter
purpose	the use or reason for this form of writing
audience	the expected readers of the text
things to know	important information about the form of writing
sentence starters	the opening clause of the sentence; these sentence starters are shown in italics in the examples of each form of writing
useful vocabulary	some suggested language that is characteristic of, or commonly used in, the form of writing
modality	expressing ideas such as *probability, certainty, frequency,* and *importance* using additional words to extend the main verb
glossary	definitions of other key words used in this book (see pages 51 to 53)

briefing note/paper

purpose

to keep decision-makers informed about issues for which they are responsible

audience

senior managers within the organisation

things to know

A briefing note is a short paper that quickly and effectively informs a decision-maker about an issue.

A good briefing note presents complex information in a short, well-structured document. Longer briefing notes should include headings.

Briefing notes include the date of preparation and the name and contact details of the author.

sentence starters

This briefing note is about ...
It has been written in preparation for ...<*event*>
The background to this issue is ...
A brief chronology is ...
The relevant facts/issues are ...
The current situation is ...
There is an opportunity to ...
...<*name*> is likely to argue that ...
It is suggested that if asked about ... you respond by ...
If ...<*name*> seeks ..., it is suggested that ...
Some possible questions you may be asked and suggested responses are ...
Whilst ...<*name*> may propose that ..., it is important to consider that ...
The following people have been consulted ...
The implications for ... are ...
Key considerations are ...
The options are ...
You may wish to ...
It is recommended that ...
The next step is to ...

useful vocabulary

act/action
background
choose/choice
considerations
could
decide/decision
events
implications
issues
might
perhaps
provide/provision
recommend/recommendation
reply
response
should
suggest/suggestion

example

Chief Executive Officer

APRIL MANAGEMENT MEETING

This briefing note is about Item 3 on the agenda of the April management meeting. *The background to this issue is* the forthcoming retirement of May Smith. *There is an opportunity to* review the skills and duties of the position before advertising for a replacement. Charles Gray *is likely to argue* that May's replacement should be familiar with the MYOB accounting package. However, a higher salary might be needed to attract an applicant with these additional skills. There is no provision for salary increases in the company's annual budget. *If* Charles *seeks* such a change, *it is suggested that* you ask him to finance the increased salary by making savings elsewhere in his departmental budget.

Teresa Green
Financial Controller
ph: (07) 6543 2123; email: tgreen@xyz.com.au
30 March 2016

business plan

purpose

to explain a business's goals and how they will be achieved; often in the context of starting a new business or expanding into a new area of business activity

audience

banks, prospective investors, managers, accountants, government agencies

things to know

A business plan is an extended explanation, covering what things the business will do, how the business will do those things, and why things will be done that way.

sentence starters

... offers its customers/clients ...

The business will capitalise on the strong/growing demand for ... by ...

With our plan to ..., the business will take advantage of recent trends in ...

... will position itself as ...

The mission/aim/objective of ... is ...

The major investors/shareholders/managers are ...

Key managers/personnel/board members/advisors include: ...

... is a registered company/partnership/sole trader/not for profit organisation located in ...

The property is located in ..., with the advantages of ...

The objectives for the first year of operations are ...

This will be achieved by ...

... will focus its marketing activities on ...

The start-up expenses totalling $... include ...

The average monthly costs of ... requires sales of ... to break-even.

The assets/equipment/inventory that will need to be purchased, for a total cost of $..., include ...

Projected sales/cash flow/profits for the next three years are ...

Funding for the business comes from ...

Our market research shows that ...

Our direct competition will be ...

... will price its products/services competitively as follows: ...

useful vocabulary

advantage/strength	fit out	mission statement	realistic
balance sheet	focus	objective	revenue/income/sales
break-even	industry leader	opportunity	risk
budget/budgeted	inventory/stock	people/personnel	risk management
client/customer	investment/investors	plan/strategy	shareholders
competition/competitor	key performance indicators	profit and loss statement	start-up
costs/expenses	manager/manage/management	purpose	threat/weakness
financial	marketing		

example

A business plan is usually lengthy – too long to show a full example here. However, a list of the commonly used headings is shown.

BUSINESS PLAN OUTLINE

Executive summary: *write this last*

Business overview: *what the organisation does, legal framework and ownership, when founded, results to date, organisation, management team*

Industry analysis: *the target market, competitors, market size*

Customer analysis: *who they are, why they need the product/service*

Competition: *direct and indirect competitors, competitive advantage (SWOT analysis)*

Marketing plan: *product/services, pricing, how to reach customers, how the product/service will be delivered*

Operations plan: *location, use of technology, equipment needed, start-up plan for business/ new product/new service, staffing, key performance indicators, risks and how to manage them*

Management plan: *key managers, background and skills*

Financial plan: *sales forecasts, projected profits/ losses, cash flow and balance sheet*

Appendices: *supporting documents*

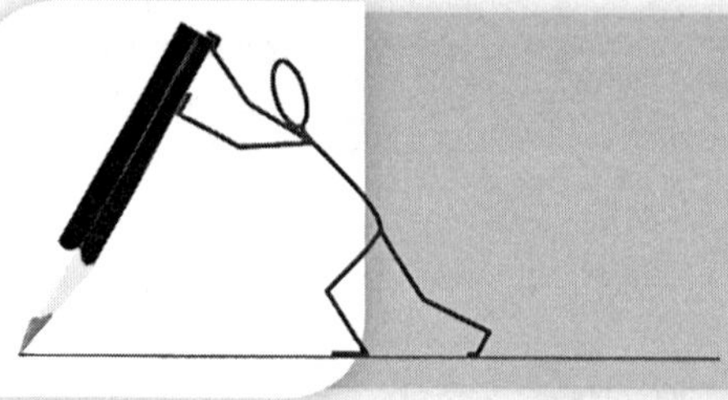

email

purpose

to provide information, persuade, motivate, or promote

audience

individuals, groups, and organisations, both internal and external

things to know

As emails are often used in place of letters and memos, the information about writing letters (pages 12 and 13) and memos (pages 20 and 21) is also relevant.

Generally, it is easier, more efficient, and more environmentally friendly to email. However, printed mail (also called snail mail) often commands more respect and attention than email. Emails are unsuitable when sending an object, for example a book, catalogue, or product sample.

***Never put anything in an email that you would not be comfortable with anyone reading,** because: (a) once sent, emails can be forwarded to others without the knowledge of the author; (b) as most organisations back up their computer systems regularly, emails can be retrieved even if they have been deleted by the users; and (c) system administrators are often able to access anyone's email accounts.*

When forwarding an email to a new recipient, check that earlier emails (shown below the current email) are suitable for the new recipient. Take care using the 'Reply All' button. Ensure you do really want to send a copy to everybody listed.

Correct spelling, grammar and punctuation matter in business emails.

sentence starters

The purpose of this email is to ...

As requested, this email is to remind you of ...

Following our recent conversation ...

Attached is a copy of ...

The information can be found at this URL/by following this link: ...

I have attached a copy of ... to this email and have forwarded the original through the mail.

I am writing to ...

This email is to confirm ...

I am pleased to provide/confirm/attach ...

As discussed, ...

Thank you for ...

useful vocabulary

act/action	commercial in confidence	Hello	reply/reply all
as soon as possible	confidential	Hi	sender
attach/attachment	discussed/discussion	immediate	snail mail
attention	email (e-mail)	Kind regards	thank you
bcc (blind copy to)	forward	link	urgent
best wishes	greetings	please/pleased	URL (uniform resource locator)
cc (copy to)	good morning/afternoon	recipient	when possible

example

Send	From	Susan Harris
	To ...	All new employees
	Cc ...	Operation manager
	Bcc	
	Subject	Writing company emails

Hi everyone

Welcome to the company. *The purpose of this email is* to provide you with an example of how our company would like you to format business emails.

Always start with a descriptive subject line that tells the recipient what the email is about. Opening emails with 'Dear ...' and closing with 'Yours faithfully/sincerely' is generally thought to be outdated. We prefer the more friendly *'Hi'* followed by the recipient's name.

Keep business emails professional. However, they can be semi-formal (for example, to a colleague in the company) or formal (for example, to a new customer). Spelling, grammar and punctuation matter. Avoid emoticons, text language and frequent abbreviations. *Please* do not use capital letters, underlining, changes in font type or size, or many exclamation marks, as they can be interpreted as shouting.

Keep emails short. They should conclude with a signature block. *Please* set up an automatic signature block for yourself similar to the one I have used in this email.

Thank you.

Susan Harris

HR Manager, XYZ Company
http://xyzco.com.au
PO Box 123, Summer Hill, QLD, 4567
Ph: (07) 6543 2123; email sharris@xyz.com.au

envelope

purpose

to provide information required for delivery

audience

post office, courier, receptionist, recipient

things to know

Documents in print form often require a suitably addressed envelope. Envelopes can be addressed by printing the address block (a) directly on the front of the envelope; (b) in a particular location on the letter, which is then folded so the address can be seen through a window in the envelope; or (c) onto a label that is affixed to the envelope.

The address block is placed on the centre front of the envelope, beginning approximately halfway down the envelope and one-third of the way across. Australia Post's preferred format for the address is to have no punctuation and the last line to include suburb, state and postcode written in block capitals with two spaces between each element.

Sender's details are required only if the envelope is not pre-printed with the sending organisation's name and address.

It is the policy of some organisations that the receptionist or registry opens all mail addressed to the organisation, regardless of the name on the envelope, unless the envelope is marked 'personal' or 'private and confidential'.

useful vocabulary

address	confidential	postcode	sender
addressee	GPO (General Post Office)	PO (Post Office)	surface mail
airmail	in-confidence	private and confidential	to be opened by addressee only
attention	personal	recipient	urgent
by hand			

example

XYZ Company Pty Ltd
PO Box 123
Summer Hill QLD
4567

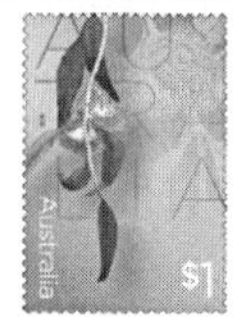

essential

CONFIDENTIAL — *optional*

Production Manager — *optional*
Seaglove Manufacturing Pty Ltd — *essential*
GPO Box 2345 — *essential*
BRISBANE QLD 4001 — *essential*
AUSTRALIA — *if overseas*

Attention: Mr P W Jones — *optional*

file note

purpose

to record the details of a discussion, action or incident, for information in the future, when there is no suitable existing form or template

audience

individuals and groups inside the organisation

things to know

A file note commences with the date and the name and/or title/position of the author. There is no recipient. It includes a descriptive subject line. A file note should be personally signed by the author because it can be used as evidence in court.

A file note should not be a substitute for existing reporting arrangements or forms, for example health, and safety accident and incident reports.

sentence starters

This note records details about/an incident where/a complaint from/a telephone conversation with/...

...‹*name*› advised/suggested that ...

I pointed out that ...

To conclude, ...

The incident/conversation was witnessed by ...

This action was taken following instructions from ...

useful vocabulary

act/action	conversation	incident	matter
attention	discuss/discussion	instruct/instruction	record of
complaint	in person	issue	telephone

example

A FILE NOTE

17 July 2016

RECORD OF CONVERSATION – INTERNET PROBLEMS

This note records a telephone conversation with 'John' from Telco Corp (ph 131735) whom I contacted in relation to the poor internet service we have been experiencing since May this year. John *advised that* there have been problems with the service in this area since their equipment was upgraded in late April.

He suggested that we continue to complain whenever the service is unacceptable, document the problems, and seek compensation. *I pointed out* to him *that* a functioning internet service was more important to us than compensation.

He arranged for a technician to make yet another visit next week.

J F Bryant

June Bryant
Office Manager

letter

purpose

to provide information, persuade, motivate, or promote

audience

individuals outside the organisation, people working in other organisations

things to know

A letter can be the first contact an organisation has with the public, and they will form opinions about the organisation based on what it says and how it is written. It is essential that the writer uses formal language, with perfect presentation, and correct spelling, grammar and punctuation.

A letter is printed on the organisation's letterhead and starts with the date and, optionally, a reference number or code, followed by the name and address of the recipient. A salutation ('Dear ...,') appears on the next line. Letters do not usually have a subject line or headings, although they can do, they are always signed by the sender, usually by hand.

If the recipient is known to you, the salutation should use their name (either first name or title and surname) and the letter should close with 'Yours sincerely'. Otherwise, the salutation should be 'Dear Sir/ Madam' and the letter should close with 'Yours faithfully'.

sentence starters

Thank you for ...

I am writing to enquire about/apologise for/confirm that/comment on ...

We/I recently wrote to you about ...

I refer to your letter of ..., reference number ..., concerning ...

I refer to our telephone conversation of ... about ...

Would you possibly ...?

I am delighted/pleased to ...

We would like to inform you about ...

In answer to your question/inquiry about ...

Attached/enclosed is a copy of a document/report about ...

Please telephone me on ... if you have further questions/require further assistance.

I/We look forward to ...

I would appreciate your immediate attention to this matter.

In conclusion, I reiterate that ...

We hope that we may continue to rely on your valued custom.

I regret any inconvenience that we have caused.

useful vocabulary

attach/attachment	finally	kindly	thank you
Dear	I am afraid that	please	unfortunately
enclose/enclosure	in conclusion	refer/reference	Yours faithfully/sincerely

example

Bookcorp Pty Ltd
PO Box 134
BELLAMY QLD 4167

21 October 2016

Mr P Toft
45 Scott Street
ALSTON QLD 4567

Dear Mr Toft

Thank you for your telephone inquiry of 13 October asking for our most recent catalogue.

I am pleased to enclose the latest information. You may find it convenient to join our mailing list so you can receive future catalogues as soon as they are issued. *Please* register online at http://bookcorp.com.au.

We look forward to welcoming you as our customer.

Yours sincerely

Pamela French

Pamela French
Marketing Officer

media release

purpose

to announce an event, service, product or change, or to share a newsworthy story about the organisation

audience

press and/or media organisations (directly), members of the public (indirectly)

things to know

A media release is the quickest and easiest way for an organisation to get free publicity.

Write as a journalist would – in third person; avoid saying 'I' or 'we' unless it is in a direct quote. Avoid sales-pitch language, jargon and excessive adjectives. Be brief – one page is best.

Media releases generally include background information about the company or organisation featured in the media release, and the details of a contact person (company name, phone/fax, email, physical/postal address).

sentence starters

For immediate release

Hold for release until ...‹*time, date*›

...‹*business name*› today introduced/announced ...

'... ‹*quote*›,' said ... ‹*name*›, ... ‹*position in the organisation*›

...‹*position, name*› said, '...‹*quote*›'

The new ...‹*product/service*› features/offers ...

...‹*product*› goes on sale today in ...

More information is expected to be released ...

Tickets for ...‹*event*› can be purchased at ...

...‹*organisation*› started trading in ..., and today offers ...

useful vocabulary

announce/ announcement	embargo	in future	source
dateline	headline	quote	

example

MEDIA RELEASE

FOR IMMEDIATE RELEASE:

BLACK DOGS NOT WELCOME IN BUNKUM

Bunkum, Tasmania – April 1 2016

The Bunkum Town Council *today announced* it will no longer register black dogs because they are too difficult to see at night.

The Mayor, Mr Peter Hoakes, said, 'Statistics show that black dogs are the cause of 34% of night-time car accidents and 15% of household accidents.'

In future, all dogs that are more than half black must have their fur bleached white before they can be registered.

The Council has arranged for the 'Hair for You' salon to offer a discounted hair colouring service for dogs with dark hair.

Dr Heir of the Bunkum Hospital welcomed the initiative. 'It will reduce the demand for emergency services at night,' he said.

The Mayor expects other towns will be quick to adopt this innovative public safety measure.

Contact: Ms Fi Doe, Dog Control Officer, Bunkum Town Council, fi.doe@bunkum.gov.au, phone (03) 4567 4321

meeting notice (agenda)

purpose

to advise of the arrangements for a meeting and the intended business of that meeting

audience

those invited to the meeting

things to know

Agendas for meetings are written in present tense and third person. They use bulleted or numbered points in list form.

Items are written briefly.

sentence starters

Meeting of ...‹*committee, organisation*› to be held at ...‹*location*› at ...‹*time*› on ...‹*date*›

Confirmation of minutes

Business arising from minutes

Reports from ...

Notice of motion that ...

Any other business

Date and time of next meeting

useful vocabulary

action	executive	notice of motion	second/seconder
agenda	general meeting	propose/proposer	secretary
annual general meeting (AGM)	item	regrets	special general meeting
apologies	meeting	report	subcommittee
attendance	minutes/minuted	rescind/rescission	treasurer
chairman	motion	resolved/resolution	working party
committee			

example

AGENDA

***Meeting of the Management Committee to be held in* Room A21 *at* 3 pm *on* 15 July 2016**

1. Attendance
2. Apologies
3. Announcements
4. *Confirmation of minutes*
5. *Business arising from minutes*
6. *Reports from* office holders
   - 6.1 Report on accident occurring on 3 July 2016 (Health and Safety Officer)
   - 6.2 Recruitment plans for 2017 (HR Officer)
7. New business
   - 7.1 *Notice of motion* that motion number 3.1 carried at the previous meeting be rescinded (Peters/Smith)
   - 7.2 Reorganisation of Finance Department
   - 7.3 End-of-year party arrangements
8. *Any other business*
9. *Date and time of next meeting*

meeting record (minutes)

purpose

to permanently record the business transacted and resolutions adopted at official meetings of an organisation, in a formal and detailed manner

audience

individuals attending the meeting; groups within the organisation

things to know

Minutes of meetings are written in past tense, third person and predominantly passive voice. Meetings require a minimum number of members, called a 'quorum', to be present in order to proceed. The size of the quorum varies depending on the organisation's rules.

Commonly used headings include:

- *Attendance*
- *Apologies*
- *Announcements*
- *Confirmation of minutes*
- *Business arising from minutes*
- *Reports from office holders*
- *New business*
- *Any other business*
- *Date and time of next meeting*
- *Closure of meeting*

sentence starters

Minutes of the [special] meeting of ...‹*committee, organisation*› held at/in ...‹*location*› on ...‹*date*›.

The Chairman opened the meeting at ...‹*time*›.

Those attending were ...

Apologies were received from ...

Moved (...‹*proposer*›, ...‹*seconder*›) that the minutes [as corrected] be accepted as a true and correct record of the previous meeting. Carried.

...‹*person*› asked/reported/stated/explained/announced that ... (see alternatives to said on page 49)

Moved (...‹*proposer*›, ...‹*seconder*›) that ...‹*text of motion*›. Carried/failed.

Moved (...‹*proposer*›, ...‹*seconder*›) that the motion be amended by adding/deleting the words ...‹*words to be added or deleted from the text of motion*›. Carried/failed.

It was agreed/resolved that ...

The Chairman ...

The motion lapsed for the want of a seconder.

The motion, as amended, was put and carried.

‹*Person*› asked that his/her dissent to the motion be recorded in the minutes.

General discussion followed. Key points included: ...

The next meeting will be held at ...‹*time*› on ...‹*date*› in/at ...‹*location*›.

The meeting closed at ...‹*time*›.

useful vocabulary

also see alternatives to said on page 49

abstain/abstention	committee	motion	second/seconder
act/action	confirmation of minutes	move	secretary
agenda	executive	on notice	special general meeting
appointed	failed	propose/proposer	subcommittee
annual general meeting (AGM)	general meeting	quorum	treasurer
apologies	item	record	unanimous
attendance	lapsed	recuse	working party
carried	meeting	report	
chairman	minutes/minuted	resolved/resolution	

example

Minutes of the special meeting of the Management Committee held in Room A21 on 27 August 2016

The Chairman opened the meeting at 3 pm, explaining that the special meeting had been called to discuss the car accident on 26 August 2016.

1. *Those attending were* Tom Delaney (Chairman), Freda Ball, Peter Gain, Nerida Smith (Secretary).
2. *Apologies were received from* Gail Chapman.
3. Accident occurring on 23 August 2016.

Freda Ball explained the circumstances of the accident in the company vehicle in which Andy Jones was seriously injured. *It was agreed that* Freda Ball would act as the company representative assisting Mr Jones, his family and the hospital.

Motion (Ball/Gain) *that* Tom Delaney be appointed as the company representative to assist the Police with their enquiries. *Carried unanimously.*

The Chairman asked Nerida Smith to ensure that counselling is available for any company employee.

4. Any other business: None
5. *The meeting closed at* 3:45 pm.

memorandum (memo)

purpose

to share information, advise of changes, explain procedures, report on activities, seek permission, or request/recommend action

audience

individuals or groups within the same organisation

things to know

A memo is used by an organisation for internal communication. It is usually typed, but uses a simple form of presentation to save cost.

A memo can be less formal than a business letter, but still should be professional and brief.

A memo commences with the date, the name, and/or the title/position of the sender and of the recipient. It includes a descriptive subject line and longer memos may have section headings.

In many organisations, memos are now transmitted by email rather than on paper (hard copy). However, the principles of writing a memo apply regardless of the form of transmission.

sentence starters

You asked me to ...
In answer to your question about ...
This memo informs you of/asks about/confirms that/comments on/advises that ...
After receiving information from ..., I ...
I refer to our telephone conversation of ... about ...
We need to ...
Please confirm that ...
I would be pleased to ...
Thank you for your assistance in ...
Attached is a document/report about ...
In conclusion, I reiterate that ...
Please contact me on ... if you have further questions/require further assistance.
I will see you at the meeting on ...
Having explained ...,
I/we would appreciate ...
I regret any inconvenience that I have caused.
Finally, to conclude ...

useful vocabulary

act/action	attention	please	urgent
as soon as possible	immediate	thank you	when possible
attach/attachment	memo/memorandum		

example

MEMO

24 February 2016

To: All new employees
From: Susan Harris, Human Resources Manager

How to write a memo

You asked me to provide you with an example of the preferred memo format used within our company.

The memo should commence with a sentence about its purpose. The body of the memo might include two to four paragraphs succinctly outlining the details. If it is a longer memo, headings should be included to guide the reader through the document.

Finally, the memo should include a summary paragraph, restating the main points. It concludes with the action required by the reader or writer. A memo is not usually signed.

Having explained the preferred memo style, *we would appreciate* it if you could follow this style for all communications within the company.

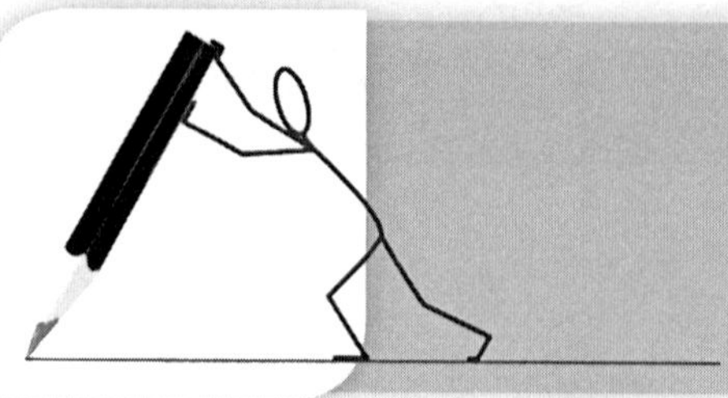

newsletter

purpose

to provide regular information about the activities and achievements of the organisation and/or individuals associated with the organisation

audience

individuals, groups and organisations within and outside the organisation

things to know

A newsletter can be written for customers or clients as a form of marketing, or for staff to inform them of what is happening in the organisation. It focuses on essential information and good news. Bad news should be delivered in a more personal manner.

Articles start with a heading and end with the details of who to contact for more information, if needed. Language choices can be more informal to achieve a 'chatty' style similar to a magazine article.

Simple newsletters including text and images can be prepared in a word processing program, whilst more complex newsletters can be formatted using desktop publishing software or templates.

Mailing lists for newsletters should be regularly maintained and updated. It is important to follow relevant anti-spamming regulations which prohibit the sending of unsolicited commercial electronic messages.

sentence starters

Welcome to our newsletter for ...‹*month/time period*›
It's been a busy week/month/term at ...‹*organisation name*› as we ...
This month/over the past few weeks we have been working on ...
Congratulations to ...
Please note/ensure that ...
Please ensure that/be aware that on ...‹*date*› ...
...‹*event*› will occur on ...‹*date*›.
The procedure for ... will change to ... on ...
We are pleased/excited/delighted to announce that ...
New products available this month include ...
Special offers for this month are: ...
New staff commencing this month are ...
We are pleased to welcome/introduce ...
We apologise for ...
The deadline for items for the next newsletter/edition is ...

useful vocabulary

announce/announcement	discount	notice	reduced
arrive/arrival	editor	offer	sale
award	information	office circular	service
best wishes	introduce	opportunity	spam
catalogue	invite/invitation	prize/prize winner	special
change	maintenance	procedure	staff
congratulations	new	product	welcome
contact	newsletter		

example

XYZCO PTY LTD

STAFF NEWSLETTER – 29 FEBRUARY 2016

Sales Award
Congratulations to Sylvia Johns for the highest sales figures for the month of February. A fine effort. Her name will go in the end of year draw for the dinner for two at Sails restaurant.

Fire Equipment Tests
The half-yearly testing of fire equipment *will occur on* Tuesday 15 March 2016. *We apologise* in advance *for* any inconvenience.
Contact: Chris Watters, Maintenance, ext 219

Easter Break – Bins
Please ensure that food scraps and waste are placed in the wheelie bin outside the building on Thursday 24 March 2016. Office bins will not be emptied during Easter break.
Contact: Ashley Peters, Office Manager, ext 248

New Arrival
If Mike Schwartz has been looking tired recently it is because his wife Belinda gave birth to Nicole Jane (3.3 kg) on 23 February. Mother and baby are well (not so sure about the father). Best wishes to all.

March Newsletter
Deadline for items for the next edition is 25 March 2016.
Contact: Freya Anderson, Editor, ext 205

proposal/ submission

purpose

to offer, apply or bid for the opportunity to receive funding, provide a product or service, or receive an award

audience

individuals or groups outside the organisation, including other organisations

things to know

A business proposal offers a particular product or service to a potential buyer or client. There are generally two kinds: solicited (submitted in response to an advertisement published by the buyer or client) and unsolicited (submitted or given out to potential customers or clients even though they did not ask for one).

Solicited proposals or submissions are often required to include a completed application form/template or particular information. They often have a deadline (date by which the information must be provided). Late submissions may be excluded or disadvantaged.

sentence starters

This submission is in response to ...

Our organisation is ..., with experience of/expertise in/specialist knowledge of ..., and staff who are qualified to ...

I/we specialise in ...

I/we can assure you of ...

To date, ...

I/we believe ...

The solution recommended for ...

The purpose of this is ...

This proposal aims to achieve the following ...

The advantages of this approach are ...

Our business is in the best position to meet your needs because ...

Our business can deliver this result on time and within budget, by ...

The following people in our organisation have the qualifications/skills/knowledge to help you achieve this result: ...

Your business will benefit from our solution/process/product/service by ...

We have experience in this type of work; for example ...

We have previously worked with ..., assisting them to ...

But don't just rely on our word – listen to the companies we have previously worked with: ...‹*list of past clients*›

I/we look forward to/would appreciate the opportunity to ...

I/we have attached ...

useful vocabulary

apply/application	fee summary/schedule	price	solutions
budget	financial breakdown	propose/proposal	submission
costs/benefits	innovative	reasons	tender
evidence	pitch	solicited/unsolicited	unique

example

Sarah Long
23 Wilshire Street
Seahaven QLD 4829
s.long@silverforyou.com.au
0418 327 432

15 November 2016

To whom it may concern

My name is Sarah Long. I am a local artisan making silver jewellery. *To date*, I have sold my products at local markets, but would like to expand into the retail market.

I specialise in unique, bold, chunky pieces that make a statement about the wearer. *I believe* my pieces would complement the fashions sold in your shop and have a similar target market. *I can assure you of* a guaranteed supply of my products.

I have attached some photographs of my recent work. I can also make pieces to order.

I would appreciate the opportunity to call on you to show you my products and discuss a sale or return arrangement. My contact details are shown above.

I look forward to the opportunity to work with you.

Yours sincerely

Sarah Long

report

purpose

to provide information to, solve problems for, and assist in decision making by the organisation or its clients, for example, feasibility study, project report, financial report, technical report, case study, annual report

audience

managers within the organisation; regulatory bodies; client organisations; other individuals or groups outside the organisation

things to know

Information provided in business reports needs to be easy to find and written so the reader can understand it. Consequently, reports are divided into sections labelled with headings and sub-headings. Detailed information that would clutter the body of the report is placed in appendices.

sentence starters

Studies have/this study has shown that ...
The main reasons for ...
The purpose of this report/chapter/section is to ...
This report/chapter/section discusses ...
We consulted ...
It is important because ...
The costs involved include ...
When asked for/why/how, ...
The data/information collected show(s) that ...
The data/findings/conclusions/recommendations can be considered in two/three categories ...
Figure/table ...‹*number*› shows that ...
Based on this information/the table/the findings, ...
The evidence for this statement is ...
An example of this is ...
After considering ...
Other options are ...
Recommendations for ... include ...

useful vocabulary

achieve/achievement	document/ documentation	marketing	realistic
alternative	evaluate/evaluation	measurable	recommend/ recommendation
appendix/appendices	evidence	methods	scope
balance sheet	expenditure	objective	specific
best practice	financial	option	technical
budget	focus	organise	terms of reference
client	income	profit and loss statement	viable/viability
data	information	purpose	

example

A business report is usually lengthy – too long to show a full example here. However, a list of the headings commonly used is shown.

BUSINESS REPORT OUTLINE

Title Page: report title, author(s) name and title, organisation's name, preparation date

Executive Summary: overview of the introduction, body, and conclusion (3 pages maximum)

Table of Contents: list of sections with page numbers

Introduction: purpose, terms of reference/ scope, outline of report's structure

Body: information collected, findings, discussion of findings, with headings and sub-headings

Conclusion: major inferences drawn from the discussion, recommendations

References: listed in alphabetical order by author

Appendix: detailed information in support of the other sections

speech/ presentation

purpose

to inform and/or entertain in a spoken presentation

audience

a group of listeners, who might be attending the occasion in person or watching/listening to a recording

things to know

A speech is an important way of promoting an organisation and/or the ideas it supports. Good speeches require much preparation. The speaker may support the speech with a visual presentation.

The tone of the speech should suit the occasion. An informative speech delivered to a conference will have a different tone from an entertaining after-dinner speech.

The speaker may use a script in which every word is written down. However, this can result in a very stilted delivery style. Alternatively, confident speakers may use speaking notes, which summarise in point form the important parts of the speech. Speaking notes result in a more natural presentation.

sentence starters

Good morning/afternoon/evening ...

Thank you, ...‹*name*› for that kind introduction ...

I acknowledge the ... people, the Traditional Owners of the land where we meet, and pay respects to their Elders, past, present and emerging.

Before I continue I would like to acknowledge ...‹*names*› who are here in the audience.

I was pleased to receive an invitation to speak today because ...

I have been asked/plan to speak about ...

My background is ...

My company is/does ...

I first became interested in this issue when ...

Many of you will know that ...

I want to emphasise that ...

A funny thing ...

So, in conclusion ...

In the few minutes remaining, I would be pleased to take any questions about ...

Should any of you want to know more, I can be contacted on ...

useful vocabulary

acknowledge	elders	invite/invitation	presentation
address	good morning/afternoon/ evening	keynote	question
anecdote/story	greeting	kind	script
chairman	humour/humorous	lecture	speak/speech
conclude/conclusion	information	opportunity	speaking notes
congratulations	introduce/introduction	pleased	traditional owners
contact			

example (speaking notes)

SPEECH ON EFFECTIVE SPEECHMAKING

SPEAKING NOTES

Greet audience; acknowledge Chair and people in the audience; acknowledge Traditional Owners; introduce self

Introduction: What is the speech about; use a 'hook' to make the audience want to listen

Body: What makes a good speech:

- Preparation – what do you want to say?
- Consider purpose and audience
- Information presented in a way that interests the audience; plenty of examples
- Use of appropriate humour
- Don't speak too quickly; include pauses
- Short sentences, simple vocabulary
- Informal language choices to create conversational style
- Don't sound as if every word is being read: use changes in emphasis, pace and intonation
- Not too many overhead slides; only a few points per slide; don't read them to the audience
- Make sure you can pronounce any tricky words and names – rehearse them out loud
- Not too long – rehearse the timing

Conclusion: summary; link back to the opening 'hook'

Thanks: to Chairman and whoever invited you to speak, but not the audience (the audience should thank you)

Questions: from the audience (if appropriate to the occasion and sufficient time)

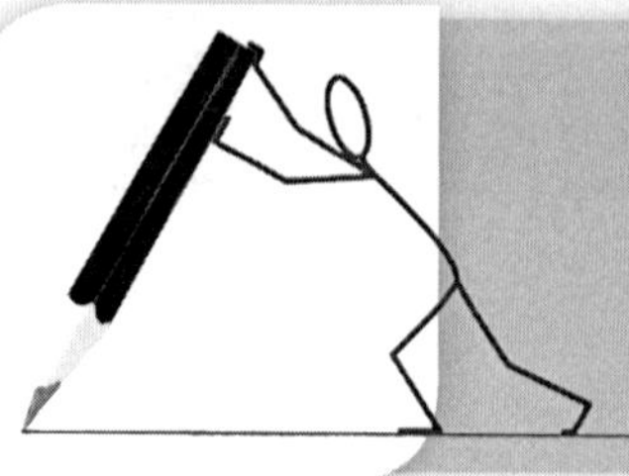

employment (job) application

purpose

to persuade a prospective employer of a person's suitability for employment in the organisation

audience

The person who, or committee (selection panel) that, selects new employee(s); the human resources section of an organisation

things to know

A written job application is often the first contact a potential employer has with you, and they will form opinions about you based on what and how you write. It is essential that spelling, grammar and punctuation are correct, and the presentation is perfect. A personalised application is more effective than one that you have paid someone to write for you.

Job applications start with a short covering letter, formatted as a business letter. The covering letter should provide enough information to persuade the busy reader to read the rest of the application.

*Additional information is provided in attachments. They may include: a completed application form; a response to the selection criteria (pages 36 and 37); a resume or curriculum vitae (pages 38 and 39); copies (**not originals**) of qualifications; and written references (pages 34 and 35).*

Job advertisements often have a deadline (date by which the application must be received). Late applications may be excluded or disadvantaged in the selection process.

sentence starters

I wish to be considered for the position of ...

Because of my previous experience and qualifications ...

The [particular] strength(s) I can bring to the position is/are ...

I am keen for an opportunity to work in/to learn about ...

I enclose ...

... are included in my resume.

As this will be my first position since completing my education, I am looking forward to ...

I am very interested in working for your company because ...

I have worked in a voluntary capacity as ...

I believe that ...

My career objective is to ...

I am available for an interview at ...

Thank you for considering ...

I look forward to hearing from you.

useful vocabulary

also see alternative action verbs on page 48

ability	collegiate	include	selection criterion (singular)/criteria (plural)
achieve/achievement	duty statement	job description	supervise/supervision/ supervisor
advise (verb)/advice (noun)	education	position	training
asset	enclose/enclosure	promote/promotion	vocation/vocational
attached/attachment	experience in	referee/reference	work
career opportunity	expertise in	resume/curriculum vitae/ cv	Yours sincerely

example

Mr G Gilhooley
XO Restaurant
Watford QLD 4825
3 May 2016

Dear Mr Gilhooley

I wish to be considered for the position of sous-chef advertised in the Herald newspaper yesterday. *I enclose,* as requested in the advertisement, a completed application form, a copy of my Certificate III as Chef, a detailed statement relating to the selection criteria, and my resume, including the names of three referees.

I am keen for the opportunity to work in your restaurant. *Because of my previous experience and qualifications*, I am able to prepare the full range of dishes served in a-la-carte restaurants. *The particular strength I can bring to the position* is my conviction that every dish leaving the kitchen must be of the highest quality. *I believe that* I would be an asset to the kitchen team.

My contact details are included in my resume. I am available for an interview on any morning.

Thank you for considering my application.

Yours sincerely

J Rice

John Rice

job advertisement

purpose

to publicise and provide information about an employment opportunity with an organisation

audience

prospective employees of an organisation

things to know

A job advertisement (paper or online) should entice applicants with positive statements about the advantages of the job, the benefits of the position, the desirability of working for the organisation, and future opportunities. It is usually addressed to the applicant using words such as 'you' and 'your'.

A job advertisement may be accompanied by a link to further information including: details of the organisation; job title; salary and benefits; hours of work; location; key responsibilities and duties; essential and desirable qualifications, training, skills, and/or experience; selection criteria (see pages 40 and 41); contact details for inquiries; closing date for applications; how to apply; and an application form.

The advertisement should avoid suggesting that the applicant should be of a particular appearance, gender, race, age, or religion.

sentence starters

A large/small/innovative/etc. company in the ... industry is looking for ...

... is a ... organisation concerned with/operating in ...

This is a ... role for a ... person who ...

Reporting to ..., your primary role is to ...

As ... you will have responsibility for ...

With duties including ..., you will utilise your ... skills in ...

The ... aspect of your role will include ...

... will keep you challenged and busy.

A key requirement of the role is ...

You will work in partnership with ...

You will be integral to ...

To be successful in this role you must ...

If you are a ... person and want to ..., this could be your next role.

For more information about the position/vacancy go to ... or telephone ...

Applications close on ...

useful vocabulary

also see alternative action verbs on page 48

asset	duties	opportunity	skills
background	exciting	position	successful
busy	experienced	proactive	take pride
challenging	friendly	professional	team
clients/customers	independent	proven track record	utilise
close-knit	initiative	responsible/responsibility	vacancy
collaborative/ collaboration	liaison	role	well-presented
confidential	motivated	self-starter	worthwhile
diverse			

example

RECEPTIONIST/OFFICE ASSISTANT

$25 per hour
Gold Coast
Car repairs and servicing

A large company in the car repair and servicing *industry is looking for* a friendly and proactive full-time Receptionist/Office Assistant to work in their Gold Coast branch. *With duties including* admin support (75%) and reception/secretarial (25%), *you will utilise your great* administrative and organisational *skills*. The admin support aspect of your role will include taking bookings for car servicing and using the computer-based job control system. Liaison with clients, general office administration, reception duties and assisting the manager *will keep you challenged and busy. If you are a* proactive, well-presented *person and want to* be part of a close-knit team, *this could be your next* long-term *role.*

For more information about the position go to www.carservicing.com.au/receptionist *or telephone* Ian Carmichael on 07-3454 6731.

reference

purpose

to provide a personal opinion about the suitability of a person for a particular job, or about a product or service provided by an organisation

audience

the person who, or committee (selection panel) that, selects new employee(s); prospective clients of an organisation

things to know

Negative statements in a reference can have undesirable consequences for the author. Consequently, a 'code' is used where the absence of a positive statement is interpreted negatively. For example, if an employee is regularly late to work, it is usually sufficient to say nothing about punctuality. As a general rule, favourable references contain many positive statements and can be lengthy, whereas unfavourable references contain few positive statements and can be quite short.

Refer to the person by first and last name on the first occasion, and first name thereafter.

A reference is more powerful if it includes descriptive examples to support the statements made.

The techniques of writing a reference for a person can easily be adapted to writing a review of a product or service provided by an organisation.

sentence starters

It is a pleasure to write this letter of recommendation for ...*<name>*
...*<name>* has been employed in our office as ... for ...
...*<name>* has well-developed skills in ...; for example, he/she has ...
...*<name>* shows initiative when required, but will also seek guidance when needed.
...*<name>* does an excellent job as a ...
...*<name>* is able to adapt to any situation, for example ...
...*<name's>* particular strengths are ...
...*<name>* supervises ... who, under his/her direction, is/are responsible for ...
...*<name>* is always willing to assist and has an excellent relationship with ...
On a personal level, ...*<name>* has many fine qualities, including ...
In his/her current position ...*<name>* has not had the opportunity to ..., however ...
...*<name>* is a fast learner and I am sure he/she would quickly adapt to ...
...*<name>* has chosen to seek employment elsewhere because ...
I can recommend ...*<name>* without hesitation for any position for which he/she is qualified.
...*<name>* would be a credit/asset/valuable addition to your organisation.
Since he/she has been with us ...*<name>* has ...
...*<name>* leaves our employment because ...
Please contact me on ... if you require further information.

useful vocabulary

also see alternative action verbs on page 48

ability	friendly	meets expectations	satisfactory
accurate	gets along with	meticulous	self-motivated
adaptable	grasps new concepts	no hesitation	skills
adequate	hard worker	outstanding	successful
attention to detail	helpful	performance	supervise
attitude	highly developed	personable	supportive
collaborative	honoured	pleased	team mate
collegiate	innovative	professional	timely/on time/punctual
communicates	integrity	punctual	to whom it may concern
creative	intelligent	qualifications	training
credit	keen	recommend	well-developed
delighted	knowledge of	respect/respectful	well-presented
every confidence	leader	responsible	

example

To Whom It May Concern

It is a pleasure to write this letter of recommendation for Ken Ricketts as an applicant for a position with your company. Ken *has been employed in our office as* a clerical supervisor *for* the past five years. He *leaves our employment because* he will be moving with his wife to Melbourne.

Ken *does an excellent job* in this position and is an asset to our company. He has well-developed communication skills, is extremely organised, and can work independently to tight deadlines.

Ken *supervises* four office assistants *who, under his direction, are responsible for* the office's administrative and clerical tasks. Ken manages the team effectively to maintain efficient office operations.

Ken *is always willing to assist and has an excellent relationship with* our clients. He *would be an asset to any employer and I can recommend him for any position for which he is qualified.*

Yours faithfully,

Jane Smith

Jane Smith
Operations Manager

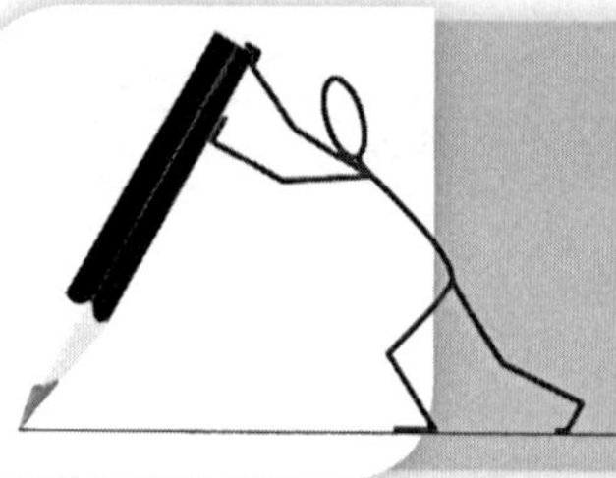

responding to selection criteria

purpose

to explain how a person meets the criteria used by an organisation to select the most suitable applicant

audience

a person who, or committee (selection panel) that, selects new employee(s); the human resources section of an organisation

things to know

Many job advertisements include details of the criteria to be used to select the successful applicant. Your written job application should explain how you fulfil those criteria.

Many applicants address selection criteria using the STAR approach. Be specific (S); identify the particular relevant task/s (T); note the action/s (A) that you undertook; and share the results (R).

People on selection committees are busy people. They do not want to read lengthy applications. You need to explain why you are the best person for the job in as few words as possible.

sentence starters

Addressing each of the selection criteria in detail, ...

Given my interest in ..., I can ...

I am able to prepare/undertake/use/operate/apply ...

I am an experienced ...

I have held the position of ...

In this role, I have participated in ...

I enjoy working as part of a team that ...

I have a proven track record over ... years doing ..., which enables me to ...

I possess qualifications/have been trained in ... that allow me to ...

I pride myself on ...

It is important to me that ...

I have delivered training to ...

My supervisors can confirm/will affirm that ...

useful vocabulary

ability
achieve/achievement
advise/advice
can-do attitude
challenging environment
collegiate
commit/commitment
contribute/contribution
create/creation
dedicate/dedication
demonstrate/demonstration
design
encourage/encouragement
experience in
expertise in
fast worker
getting the job done
goal-oriented
inspire/inspirational
lead/leadership
manage/management
mentor
perform/performance
prepare/preparation
project
promote/promotion
prompt
proven track record
quick learner
referee/reference
reliable/reliability
resume
selection criterion (singular)/ criteria (plural)
skills
strive for
strong/strength
succeed/successful
supervise/supervision
support/supportive
team/teamwork
timely/on time
undertake
well-developed
willing worker
work

example

This example illustrates how to address one selection criterion. Most vacancies have several selection criteria.

PETER DONNELLY – RESPONSE TO SELECTION CRITERIA

Criterion: Proven knowledge and implementation of Occupational Health and Safety (OH&S) practices

Response: *I have held the position of* OH&S Officer for my company since 2012. *In this role, I have participated in* 20 hours of training annually, therefore my knowledge of OH&S practices is current. *Given my personal interest in* OH&S issues, I monitor the available literature to ensure that I stay up-to-date.

Additionally, *I have delivered OH&S training to* my co-workers and used these opportunities to increase awareness of the rules and regulations relevant to their roles in the company. *It is important to me that* all employees are fully informed about, and implement, safe work practices.

I distribute weekly emails to all members of the company to ensure that they are aware of best practices. *My supervisors will affirm that* my focus on OH&S has contributed to a safe working environment. There have been no serious accidents in the company since I assumed the role in 2012.

resume/curriculum vitae (cv)

purpose

to provide factual information about an individual's personal details, qualifications and skills, work experience and other relevant activities, usually in support of an application for employment

audience

a person who, or committee (selection panel) that, selects new employee(s); the human resources section of an organisation

things to know

Resumes are highly structured documents, written in point form with many headings.

Ensure dates are continuous; that is, there are no periods of your life (personal and professional) that are unexplained.

sentence starters

I took a ...‹*duration*› break from employment to ...

In my current position my duties/responsibilities include ...

I received an award of ... for ...

useful vocabulary

awards/prizes	email address	name of employer	qualifications
career objective	employment/work experience	nationality	recreation
commendations	full name	pastimes	referees
completion date	hobbies	permanent resident	significant achievements
current duties/ responsibilities	home address	personal details	skills
curriculum vitae	home phone number	place of birth	sports
date of birth	honours	position held	summary
driver's licence	interests	postal address	visa status
education	list	previous employment	voluntary work
educational institution	mobile phone number	professional memberships/ affiliations	

example

A curriculum vitae or resume is usually two or more pages long – too long to show a full example here. However, a list of the headings commonly used is shown.

CURRICULUM VITAE – OUTLINE

Personal details: your full name, address(es), email address, phone number(s), date of birth, place of birth, nationality/visa status, driver's licence (if relevant to the job)

Qualifications/education: list of your qualifications: title, institution, date completed

Professional affiliations/memberships: list of professional or trade associations that you belong to and the membership level

Skills: list of your skills possessed

Employment/work experience: list of your previous employment: position(s) held, name of employer, dates from/to, summary of your duties/ responsibilities

Current duties/responsibilities: summary of what you do in your current job

Voluntary work: list of work done, organisation worked for, dates

Awards: list of your honours, awards, commendations and significant achievements: description, date awarded

Recreation and interests: list of your sports, hobbies, interests and pastimes

Referees: names and contact details only

selection criteria

purpose

to list the criteria used by an organisation to choose the successful applicant for a position

audience

potential job applicants; the person who, or committee (selection panel) that selects new employee(s); the human resources people of an organisation

things to know

Most job advertisements include a link to a list of the criteria to be used to select the successful applicant.

Selection criteria describe the essential and desirable qualifications, experiences, skills, knowledge and personal qualities needed for the position.

There should be no more than ten selection criteria.

sentence starters

Applications that do not address the selection criteria will not be considered.

Professional registration with ...

Recognised qualifications/certificate in ...

Completion of undergraduate/postgraduate degree in ...

Demonstrated skills in/experience with ...

Familiarity with ...

Previous work experience in ...

Proven ability to prepare/operate/manage ...

Ability to implement ...

Ability to organise and prioritise workloads with minimal supervision

Knowledge of/experience with ...

Demonstrated commitment to ...

An ability to provide accurate and timely ...

Good/excellent interpersonal skills ...

An ability to relate to people from diverse backgrounds and cultures

useful vocabulary

also see the alternative action verbs on page 48

ability	demonstrated/ demonstration	lead/leadership	selection criterion (singular)/criteria (plural)
achieve/achievement	desirable	manage/management	sensitivity to
advise/advice	detailed	manner	skills
appreciate/appreciation	environment	previous	sound
awareness	essential	prompt	succeed/successful
capacity	excellent	proven track record	supervise/supervision
challenging environment	experience in/of	quality	support/supportive
collegiate	expertise in	quick learner	team/teamwork
commitment	familiarity with	reliable/reliability	timely/on time
competence	interpersonal	responsible/responsibility	well-developed
dedicated/dedication	knowledge		

example

LIBRARY ASSISTANT

SELECTION CRITERIA

Essential

1. *Excellent interpersonal skills* and telephone manner
2. *Demonstrated commitment to* quality client service
3. *An ability to relate to people from diverse backgrounds and cultures*
4. *Experience in* a reception/office or similar environment
5. *Ability to organise and prioritise workloads with minimal supervision*
6. Excellent word processing, data entry and Internet search skills
7. *Experience with* financial record keeping, invoicing and ordering
8. *Demonstrated experience with* word processing and spreadsheet software

Desirable

9. *Previous work experience in* a library

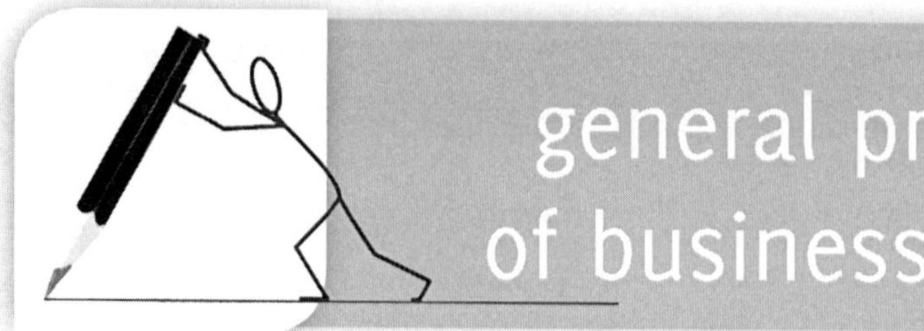

general principles of business writing

Structure

Written business communications are structured documents written with a clear purpose. A common structure for any business document is:

- **Opening** – for example, details of recipients and senders, date, reference number, subject and salutation
- **Introduction** – for example, topic, purpose, background, importance and meaning of key terms
- **Body** – for example, information, details of the problem, discussion of the issues, options available and proposed solution
- **Closing** – for example, summary, recommendations, action sought, next steps, attached/enclosed information, thank you, material referenced, acknowledgements and signature.

If the document is lengthy, the structure can be made clear to the reader (signposted) by the use of section headings.

Three-page rule

Business communications should be as brief as possible: business people are busy and time is money. In many cases one page should be sufficient, and few documents should exceed three typed pages. Where the information cannot fit into three pages, the detail, including most tables, graphs and illustrations, should be moved to attachments or appendices. A summary of that detail should be included in the main document. For example, 'market research showed that the blue logo design was preferred but the yellow design was more recognisable – see Attachment D'. However, it would be unethical to bury important information the reader *must* know in an attachment. The 'three-page rule' should allow the reader to understand the key issues after ten minutes of reading, but still be able to access additional detail if needed.

In the case of lengthy reports, an executive summary no more than three pages long should be provided.

Language choices

Brevity requires your language choices to be precise and concise, avoiding unnecessary words. You can use point form (as shown in this section) to reduce the readers' effort. Other features to consider include:

- Be professional – use a formal or semi-formal tone (depending on your audience).
- Do not confuse written language with speech – for example, most sentences will still make sense if these words are not used: absolutely, amazing, honestly, just, literally, really, stuff, very.
- Keep sentences short – 20 words is a good maximum target. If you have reached the end of a second line of text without using a full-stop, go back to investigate ways of splitting the sentence in two.

> **George Orwell's rules for clear writing**
>
> 1. Never use a metaphor, simile, or other figure of speech that you are used to seeing in print.
> 2. Never use a long word when a short one will do.
> 3. If it is possible to cut a word out, always cut it out.
> 4. Never use the passive when you can use the active.
> 5. Never use a foreign phrase, a scientific word, or a jargon word if you can think of an everyday English equivalent.
> 6. Break any of these rules sooner than say anything barbarous.

- Use adjectives sparingly – many of them are opinions, not fact – for example, *significant, substantial, insubstantial, considerable, inappropriate, appropriate, excessive, limited.*
- Do not use double negatives – for example, *the computer was not inexpensive* is better written as *the computer was expensive.*
- Avoid contractions (for example, *can't*) and clichés (for example, *sales were as flat as a pancake*).
- Choose everyday words that would be familiar to the reader – for example, *buy* instead of *purchase*, and *use* rather than *utilise*.
- Express ideas positively if you can – for example, what should be done rather than what should not be done.
- Write in active voice rather than passive voice (see the glossary on pages 51 to 53 for explanations of active and passive voice).
- Use inclusive, non-discriminatory, gender-neutral language (see page 50); do not refer to gender, religion, sexual orientation, nationality, racial group, age and physical or mental characteristics unless they are critical to the meaning of the text.

Certain words can cause problems for the future. 'Never say never', whilst a cliché, is true in business because only one example is needed to disprove a statement. Instead, replace *never* with *seldom* or *rarely*; similarly, replace *always* with *generally* or *usually*, *certain* with *highly likely*, and *impossible* with *improbable* or *unlikely*. The modality table on page 47 contains more words of this type.

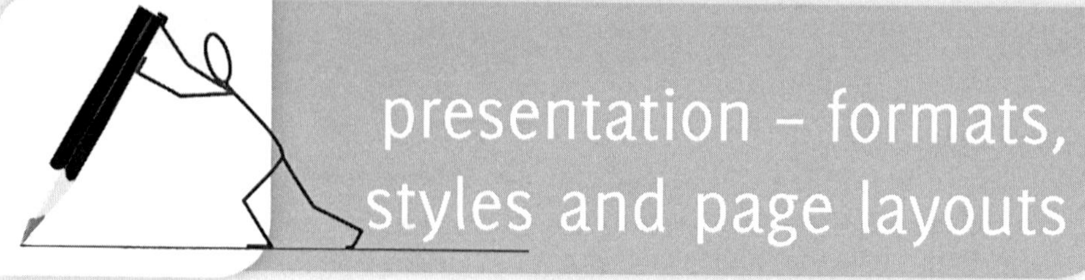

presentation – formats, styles and page layouts

The presentation of documents is important in business writing. White space on the page, created by suitable margins and skipping some lines, not only looks better, but can make it easier for the reader. The page should not be 'top-heavy', so balance the text on the page by inserting blank lines at the top of the page, if necessary.

Paper selection: The first page of some documents such as letters, newsletters, and media releases generally uses pre-printed stationery. The second and subsequent pages, and most other forms of business writing, are printed on blank paper.

Margins: A 2.5 cm margin all round works well on A4 paper. However, documents printed on letterhead may require a larger margin at the top of the page. If a document is to be bound as a book, the margin on the inside of the page is often wider to accommodate the binding.

Line spacing: Single line spacing can look cramped – line spacing between 1.08 and 1.15 points is easier to read. In some documents the lines are double or triple spaced. For example, in draft documents, extra line spacing is provided for marking in corrections, and the script of a speech has additional line spacing to make it easier for the speaker to keep track of where he/she is up to.

Names and titles: The way organisations refer to their employees in writing can vary. Some use titles or position names (for example, Human Resources Manager, Accountant, Sales Executive), and others use the employees' names (first name or initial and last name). Some organisations use abbreviations for titles/positions and initials or codes instead of names. Signature blocks generally include the name and the position of the person signing the letter (who may not be the person who drafted the letter).

Opening: When writing a letter, start with your own address on the top right-hand side (if not using pre-printed stationery), then skip one or two lines, write the date, skip four more lines and then write the name and address of the recipient. Finally, skip one or two lines before starting the salutation ('Dear ...'). In memos, start with the date, skip two lines and write 'To:' followed by the recipient(s) name(s) (addresses are not needed), skip another two lines and write 'From:' followed by the sender's name, and then skip a further two lines before writing a subject line that summarises the contents of the memo in a few words.

Body: Letters, emails and media releases usually do not use headings, but most other forms of business writing, if lengthy, require headings to assist the reader in navigating the document. All documents should be structured into paragraphs, with a blank line between paragraphs. Paragraphs may be numbered in legal and similar documents.

Closing: After writing the body of a letter or email, type the complimentary close (for example, 'Yours faithfully' or 'Yours sincerely' for a letter; 'Kind regards' for an email), leave four or five blank lines to accommodate a handwritten signature for a letter, then type the signature block, that is, the sender's name and title/position (if applicable), or insert the signature block for an email. In a letter, signature blocks should not appear by themselves on the top of a new page; if necessary, move the final paragraph to the new page. Most other forms of business writing do not have closings, but some may end with a summary of key points.

Keep text formatting simple ...

- *no italics*
- **no bold**
- no underlined words
- no words underlined twice
- no marks of overexcitement!!!!!
- no UAs
- (no ideas added in parentheses)
- "no double quotes"
- no Random Capitalisation
- NO SHOUTING
- no changes **in** font

... without a good reason.

(by the way, UA means unexplained abbreviations)

Indenting: There are a variety of methods of formatting a document. The two most common are block and indented formats. In block form, *everything* except a document title is typed flush left (the title can be centred). Examples of block format are on pages 3, 11, 13, 15, 21, 23 and 35. If using an indented format, the sender's address (if needed) and the date are written at the top, with the left edge aligned with the centre of the page. The recipient's name and address and the salutation are written flush left. The first line of each paragraph is indented by one centimetre. The complimentary close and signature lines are placed with the left edge aligned with the centre of the page (matching the date at the top of the letter). Examples of indented format are on pages 25 and 31.

Page numbering and footers: The second and subsequent pages of any document should be numbered, usually in the footer. Some organisations also include other details in a footer, such as the organisation's name and/or the title of the document.

Most organisations have a preferred style or format for business communications that all employees are asked to use (see the next section on style manuals and standard templates).

style manuals and standard templates

For many organisations, the first contact they have with their clients or customers is in written form, for example through letters, reports and newsletters. Outsiders often make judgements about an organisation based on the quality of its written communications. Correct and consistent use of writing styles, spelling, grammar and punctuation are important to all organisations.

For this reason, many organisations have style manuals or guides to ensure all written communications produced by the organisation are correct and consistent. These guides or manuals can assist writers with:

- choosing polite and respectful ways to address and write about people
- respecting equality and diversity (for example how and when to refer to gender, religion, nationality, racial group, age and physical or mental characteristics)
- selecting writing styles
- understanding words used frequently in the organisation (glossary)
- using and understanding common abbreviations and acronyms
- using the organisation's logo and stationery (including acceptable colours)
- who can sign correspondence on behalf of the organisation
- checking and proofreading of writing produced by the organisation
- selecting fonts (style and size)
- using and formatting headings and paragraphs, including numbering methods
- choosing appropriate methods of punctuation, grammar, spelling, capital letters, and showing numbers (including numerals, fractions and per cent) and measurements, especially when there are several acceptable methods
- avoiding common errors made in spelling, grammar and punctuation
- using references to acknowledge sources

Some organisations require the use of pre-prepared electronic templates and forms. They save time and ensure the consistency of written communications.

The Australian Government has produced a *Style Manual for Authors, Editors and Printers* (2002, 6th edition, John Wiley & Sons Australia Ltd, ISBN: 978-0-7016-3648-7) that is a valuable resource for all writers of business communications, especially if an organisation does not have a style manual or guide of its own. It is a useful acquisition for the libraries of all schools, training organisations, and businesses.

degrees of intensity (modality)

MODE	LOW →							HIGH
certainty	never	scarce/ scarcely	perhaps/in some cases	might/could	likely/as likely as not/in all likelihood	undoubted/ undoubtedly	inevitable/ inevitably	definite/ definitely
extent	never	scarce/ scarcely	limited	partly	general/ generally	mainly	mostly	complete/ completely
frequency	never	seldom	occasional/ occasionally	sometimes	often	usual/usually	regularly/in most cases	always
importance	desirable/ desirably	prefer/ preferably	require/ required	necessary	important/ importantly	essential/ essentially	unquestionable/ unquestionably	vital/vitally
intensity	scarce/ scarcely	slight/slightly	mild/mildly	intermittent/ intermittently	moderate/ moderately	typical/ typically	unrelenting/ unrelentingly	extreme/ extremely
obligation	may	might	perhaps	could	ought	should	have to	must
probability	impossible/ impossibly	improbable/ improbably	unlikely	possible/ possibly	likely/in all likelihood	probable/ probably	sure/surely	certain/ certainly
confidence	suspect	unreasonable/ unreasonably	doubtful/ doubtfully	moderate/ moderately	reasonable/ reasonably	plausible/ plausibly	undeniable/ undeniably	irrefutable/ irrefutably

alternative action verbs

develop	recommend	record	count	write	operate	study	lead	manage	control	contact
build	advance	attach	appraise	annotate	assemble	analyse	build	administer	approve	attend
construct	advise	circulate	calculate	compose	carry	collate	conduct	anticipate	authorise	collaborate
create	apprise	consolidate	collate	describe	drive	enquire	create	arrange	conduct	communicate
define	consult	display	compile	design	employ	estimate	encourage	assign	decide	conduct
design	counsel	document	compute	draft	handle	evaluate	ensure	close	determine	discuss
establish	counsel	file	enumerate	list	process	examine	enthuse	contract	execute	inform
formulate	endorse	find	evaluate	note	sort	explore	guarantee	control	regulate	notify
generate	interpret	furnish	reconcile	outline	use	inspect	guide	correct		participate
institute	nominate	issue	tally	report		investigate	influence	direct		refer
make	promote	itemise	total	summarise		observe	initiate	follow–up		request
organise	propose	merge				research	inspire	guide		respond
originate	put forward	note				review	manage	keep		visit
plan	submit	prepare				review	mentor	maintain		
prepare	suggest	register				sample	motivate	obtain		
produce	urge	show				survey	observe	order		
select		tabulate				test	oversee	organise		
		trace					plan	oversee		
		transfer					promote	participate		
							propose	require		
							supervise	select		
								supervise		

alternatives to 'said'

explanation

It is common practice in business communications to relate what other people have said or written. To repeatedly use the word 'said' can be tedious and unsophisticated. The list below provides some alternatives.

acknowledged
admitted
agreed
alleged
announced
argued
asserted
came to the conclusion
claimed
clarified
commented
concluded
contradicted
contended
declared
denied
described
emphasised
estimated
explained
found
indicated
made it clear
noted
offered [a well-considered solution]
offered [an alternative explanation]
opined
pleaded the case for
proposed
put forward the view
refuted
rejected
reported [the findings]
repudiated [the argument/s]
resolved
revealed
showed
stated
stressed
suggested
told
urged the reader to
vehemently denied

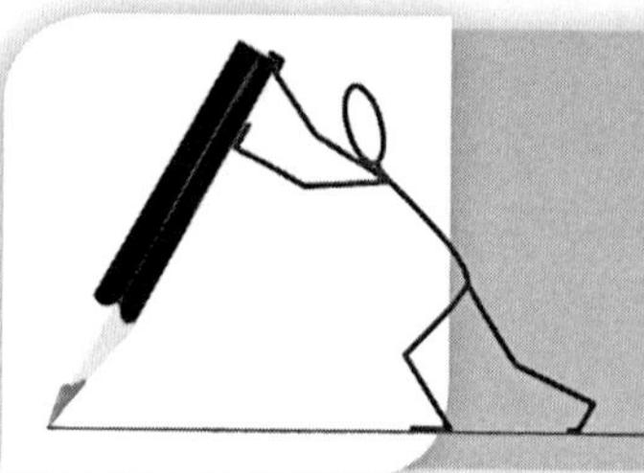

gender-neutral language

Gender-specific pronouns include *he, him, his,* and *she, her, hers*. They can suggest that a sentence applies only to people of the gender mentioned. For example, in the following sentence

Each applicant must provide details of his qualifications.

the word *his* might suggest that only males can be applicants. Gender-specific pronouns should usually be avoided in business writing.

Some ways of avoiding gender-specific pronouns are:

- Writing the sentence in the plural

  Applicants must provide details of their qualifications.

- Leaving out the pronoun

  Each applicant must provide details of qualifications.

- Using passive voice

  Details of qualifications must be provided by each applicant.

- Repeating the noun

  Each applicant must provide details of the applicant's qualifications.

- Using the pronouns for both genders

  Each applicant must provide details of his or her qualifications.

- Using the gender-neutral pronouns *you, your, yours* or *yourself*

  You must provide details of your qualifications.

- Using the gender-neutral pronouns *they, them, their, theirs,* or *themselves.*

  They must provide details of their qualifications.

However, gender-specific pronouns may be used if the sentence is about people whose genders are known, for example,

Mr Smith gave his opinion.

The mother should provide her full name on the form.

glossary

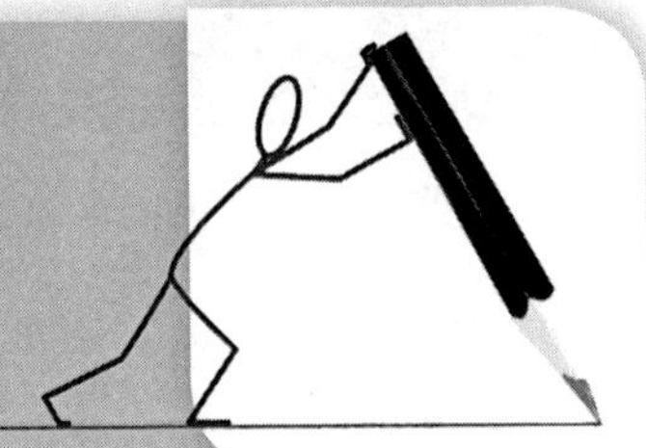

active voice
: One of the two 'voices' of verbs (see also *passive voice*). In active voice, the subject of the sentence performs the action, as in the example *Tracy wrote the letter*. 'Wrote' is an active verb here. Tracy (the subject of the sentence) performed the action of writing the letter. Since the subject is doing the action, the sentence is in active voice. Active voice is preferred in business communication because it is more direct, avoids ambiguity and is usually less wordy than passive voice.

agenda
: A plan for a meeting, including things to be discussed, propositions to be voted upon, or matters to be acted upon.

audience
: The intended readers of a document.

author
: Strictly, the author of a written work is the originator or writer of that work.

  However, in organisations there is often a team of people involved in preparing a document (in roles such as drafting, contributing ideas, checking, approving and signing). In such cases, the author is the person or organisation whose name appears on the final document. There may be several authors.

brevity
: The quality of expressing many ideas in few words.

brief (verb)
: To instruct using a short statement. It usually refers to a written statement, but it is possible to brief a person verbally.

business
: An organisation (or entity) engaged in commerce, manufacturing, or providing a service. It could be a person (sole trader), partnership, or corporation (company). Also known as a firm. Most definitions of *business* include the aim of making a profit and therefore do not include government organisations or not-for-profit organisations such as schools, churches, and charities.

  In other situations, *business* could refer to an occupation, profession or trade (e.g. 'he is in *business*'); or commercial activity (e.g. 'they do *business* together').

cf
: An abbreviation for confer, meaning *compare with.*

cliché
: A commonly used expression; a sentence or phrase that may have, at one time, been apt or amusing, but has lost originality, ingenuity, and impact by overuse.

committee
: A group of people elected or appointed to perform some service or function, such as investigating, reporting, recommending, or acting on a particular matter.

communication	The exchange of thoughts, opinions, or information by speech, writing, or signs.
complimentary close	The closing phrase used in a letter or email, e.g. *Yours sincerely* or *Kind regards*.
confidential in confidence	In privacy or secrecy; any information is limited to people authorised to access such documents.
contraction	An abbreviation of two words achieved by removing one or more letters and replacing them with an apostrophe; for example, can't, shouldn't.
curriculum vitae	A written summary of a person's experience and other qualifications, usually provided as part of a job application. *Curriculum vitae* is taken from Latin, meaning 'course of life'. The plural form (rarely used) is *curricula vitae.*
document	A written work, such as a book, article, letter, or report. If the document is stored on a computer, it may refer to the data file containing the written work.
e.g.	An abbreviation for *exempli gratia* (Latin), meaning *for example.*
et al.	An abbreviation for *et alia* (Latin), meaning *and others.*
executive	A person or group of people assigned leadership, administrative or supervisory authority in an organisation.
genre	A kind, category, or sort, especially of literary or artistic work.
i.e.	An abbreviation for *id est* (Latin), meaning *that is* or *in other words.*
inclusive language	Language that does not, directly or indirectly, exclude a section of the community.
indent	To set in from the margin.
internal (to an organisation)	Within an organisation. An email from the management to the employees of an organisation is an example of an internal communication.
key performance indicators	A type of performance measurement to evaluate the success of an organisation or of a particular activity in which it engages.
memorandum	A written message sent between two or more employees of the same organisation; often abbreviated as *memo.*
minutes	The official record of the proceedings at a meeting of a committee, working party, or other group.
organisation	An organised group of people with a particular purpose, such as a business, charity, school, or government department.
passive voice	One of the two 'voices' of verbs (see also *active voice*). In passive voice, the subject of the sentence is acted on by the verb, as in the example *The letter was written by Tracy.* Here, the subject of the sentence (*the letter*) receives the action of the verb. It is not actively doing anything, so the sentence is in passive voice. The agent or 'doer' of the action can be omitted.

glossary

proofreading To read a document to find and mark errors to be corrected.

purpose for writing The reason for preparing a written document.

quorum The minimum number of members required to be present at a meeting in order to conduct the business of the group or organisation (as determined by the organisation's governing documents, e.g. constitution, charter, or by-laws).

re An abbreviation for 'regarding'. It can be used in a heading for an email, memo, or letter to indicate the subject of the communication.

recipient The receiver of an email, letter or other communication.

salutation A greeting. The part of a letter or email that greets the recipient, for example, *Dear Mr Smith.*

selection panel A committee or group that selects new employees for an organisation.

signature block The name, title, and contact details (in the case of an email) of the sender of an email or letter. It is inserted at the end of the text of an email and below the signature in a letter

signposting Headings or statements used in a written document to indicate what is to follow.

spam Unsolicited or unwanted electronic communications.

subject line A summary in a few words to tell the reader of a document what that document is about.

SWOT analysis An evaluation of an organisation's strengths, weaknesses, opportunities and threats.

text The contents of a written or printed work. It may include prose (words), symbols, tables, and/or visual images.

typing Strictly, the action or skill of writing a document using a typewriter.

However, these days most documents are prepared using a word processing package on a computer. Thus, *typing* often includes word processing.

viz An abbreviation for *videlicet* (Latin), meaning *namely*.

word processing The action or skill of writing a document using word processing software.

word processor A computer program or system that enables the fast and efficient manipulation of text to create a document.

writing style The manner in which an author chooses to write to his or her readers. The writing style is influenced by the purpose for writing, the readers for whom the writing is intended and the writer's personality and voice.

Note that many of these words have other meanings. The meanings in this glossary are those relevant to the contents of this book.

my notes

my notes

my notes

my notes

about the authors

Patricia Hipwell M.Ed., B.Sc. Econ. (Hons), Grad. Dip. of Literacy Ed., P.G.C.E. is an independent literacy consultant for her own company, **logonliteracy**. She delivers literacy professional development to teachers in Australia, and works predominantly in Queensland schools. Patricia has specialised in assisting all teachers to be literacy teachers, especially high school subject specialists who often struggle with what it means to be a content area teacher and a literacy teacher.

Merilyn (Lyn) Carter Ph.D., M.Ed.(Research), Dip.Ed., B.Ec., operating through her business **Count on Numeracy**, is an independent consultant, providing professional development to teachers of numeracy and mathematics throughout Australia. She completed her doctoral thesis on NAPLAN numeracy testing. Lyn also works as a researcher at the Queensland University of Technology (QUT).

Patricia and Lyn have created a number of resources to assist students' literacy and numeracy development. Both consultants are available (as a cross-curricular team or individually) to provide professional development in their areas of expertise and to support the use of their recommended resources, including this one.

For further information, contact:

Patricia Hipwell
Mobile: 0429 727 313
email: pat.hipwell@gmail.com

logonliteracy

Merilyn (Lyn) Carter
Mobile: 0402 077 958
email: countonnumeracy@bigpond.com

Count on Numeracy